627 Challenging Pop Culture Trivia Questions

Seven Phoenix, Ph.D.

DEDICATION

This book is dedicated to all the pop culture trivia junkies out there.

Table of Contents

PREFACE

This volume of trivia came about for people who are seeking no-nonsense trivia questions for their own pub trivia night, personal entertainment, or to play with family and friends. These questions are essentially a "B-Side" to my main volumes of trivia, *American Pub Trivia*, of which two highly engaging and entertaining volumes have been published.

627 Challenging Pop Culture Trivia Questions

Questions 1-10

1. None of the supernatural beings from the film have any basis in real life, but Zuul, Gozer and Vinz Clortho were gods from this ancient civilization in the movie "Ghostbusters."

2. This "Jackie Brown" director was also an actor on four episodes of the TV show "Alias."

3. It's Judah Rosenthal's profession in the 1989 Woody Allen film "Crimes and Misdemeanors."

4. Which Broadway musical, first performed in 1964, had a film adaptation in 1968 with the same female lead, but Omar Sharif in the role of Arnstein?

5. What actress played Karen Hill in "Goodfellas," Dr. Jennifer Melfi in the "The Sopranos," and Diane Giacalone in "Getting Gotti?"

6. Who released the song "Where Did It All Go Wrong?" in 2000? This group was originally known as The Rain. It formed with members Paul Arthurs, Liam Gallagher, Tony McCarroll and Paul McGuigan.

7. Who released the song "Motorhead" in 1975? This English band is considered one of the early space rock groups. What's space rock? Basically, their approach to music was similar to that of Pink Floyd.

8. This 1968 Neil Simon film, later turned into a television series, centered on Felix Ungar, who decides to move in with Oscar Madison rather than kill himself.

9. What was Phoebe's favorite alias on the TV sitcom "Friends"?

10. On the original cartoon Captain Planet and the Planeteers, which one of the Planeteers wore the ring that controlled the element of water?

Answers 1-10

1. Sumerian

2. Quentin Tarantino

3. Ophthalmologist

4. Funny Girl

5. Lorraine Bracco

6. Oasis

7. Hawkwind

8. The Odd Couple

9. Regina Phalanges

10. Gi

Questions 11-20

11. What squeaky 1999 kid's film, based on a book by E.B. White, was M. Night Shyamalan credited as screenwriter for?

12. Which 1950 Broadway play was based on two short stories by Damon Runyon?

13. Who released the song "Darkness" in 2012? This artist has been inducted to the American Rock and Roll Hall, the Canadian Music Hall of Fame and the Canadian Songwriters Hall of Fame.

14. What is the name of the strip club in the HBO series "The Sopranos"?

15. This owner of Charm City Cakes and star of the Food Network show "Ace of Cakes" attempted the Guinness World Record for baking the World's Largest Cupcake in 2008.

16. "Frosty the Snowman" was first recorded by what artist in 1950, who had just scored a hit the previous year with "Rudolph the Red-Nosed Reindeer?"

17. Who released the song "Walk the Walk" in 2000? This singer, born Anne Decatur, first hit the rock charts in the mid-90s.

18. Who released the song "This I Promise You" in 2000? This American boy band formed in 1995 with the members Justin Timberlake, JC Chasez, Chris Kirkpatrick, Joey Fatone and Lance Bass.

19. What name do Niles and Frasier give to their fancy restaurant on the episode titled "The Innkeepers" on the NBC sitcom "Frasier?"

20. "Is it safe?" is a terrifying line from what 1970s film starring Dustin Hoffman, Laurence Olivier and Roy Scheider?

Answers 11-20

11. Stuart Little

12. Guys & Dolls

13. Leonard Cohen

14. Bada Bing

15. Duff Goldman

16. Gene Autry

17. Poe

18. 'N Sync

19. The Happy Brothers

20. Marathon Man

Questions 21-30

21. On the TV show "Arrested Development," what colorful musical act does Tobias want to join?

22. Which Neil Simon play opened on Broadway February 14, 1968, and told the story of Sam and Karen Nash, who were returning to their honeymoon suite on their anniversary?

23. This "Superbad" actor also plays Red Mist in the 2010 comedy film "Kick-Ass."

24. Which Broadway musical about a British schoolteacher and a King was the fifth musical written by Rodgers and Hammerstein?

25. What character is a wealthy bachelor in the musical "Hello, Dolly!?"

26. What magical weapon does Wonder Woman carry to force villains to tell the truth?

27. Who released the song "Rose" in 2000? Most of the tracks from this album were named for people that lead singer Maynard Keenan knew" "Judith", "Brena," "Thomas," "Magdalena, "Orestes."

28. What 1934 Nazi propaganda film was directed by Leni Riefenstahl?

29. Who recorded his first solo album "Takin' Off" for Blue Note Records in 1962?

30. What prize can Johnny win in his contest with the Devil in The Charlie Daniels Band song "The Devil Went Down to Georgia?"

Answers 21-30

21. Blue Man Group

22. Plaza Suite

23. Christopher Mintz-Plasse

24. The King & I

25. Horace Vandergelder

26. Golden Lasso

27. A Perfect Circle

28. Triumph of the Will

29. Herbie Hancock

30. Golden Fiddle

Questions 31-40

31. What Eastern European model joined The Velvet Underground for their debut album?

32. What comic strip follows the life of a teen-ager named Jeremy Duncan?

33. "What's with these homies dissin' my girl?" is the opening line of what Weezer song?

34. What movie does William H. Macy play a sheriff named Chappy Dent?

35. Who released the song "Cruel Summer" in 1983? Singer Sara Dallin said this song "played on the darker side: it looked at the oppressive heat, the misery of wanting to be with someone as the summer ticked by."

36. On the TV sitcom "Happy Days," the "C" stands for what last name when Fonzie uses it to refer to Richie's mother, "Mrs. C."

37. "Heaven and Heaven" is the Rock Sugar mash-up of two songs titled "Heaven," one by Canadian pop singer Bryan Adams and the other by what 80s bubblegum metal band fronted by Janie Lane?

38. Which Broadway musical about a widowed Ms. Levi won ten Tony Awards in 1964, and has had three revivals after its initial closing for a total of 2844 performances?

39. This 1993 film directed by Steven Spielberg used the tagline, "An adventure 65 million years in the making."

40. This love interest of Indiana's from "Raiders of the Lost Ark" returned in "Indiana Jones and the Crystal Skull." Oh yeah, she's also the mother of Mutt Jones.

Answers 31-40

31. Nico

32. Zits

33. Buddy Holly

34. Happy, Texas

35. Bananarama

36. Cunningham

37. Warrant

38. Hello, Dolly!

39. Jurassic Park

40. Marion Ravenwood

Questions 41-50

41. What is comic book character Namor the Sub-Mariner's position in Atlantis?

42. This oldest existing board game dating back to the Egyptian dynasties in 3500 BC was featured on an episode of the last season of Lost.

43. Britney Spears cast mate on The Mickey Mouse Club was what future Academy Award-nominated actor who went on to star in The Notebook & the Real Girl?

44. After producer Albert Ruddy got pressured by local mobsters, the word "mafia" was never mentioned in what film?

45. Who released the song "Yellow" in 2000? When writing this song Chris Martin found inspiration from a Yellow Pages telephone directory sitting in the studio.

46. Matt Groening was out of the room when the writers of The Simpsons decided to give this character the name Jeff Albertson, because Matt was obsessed with naming him Lois Lane.

47. According to the Carpenters song, "Are we really happy with this lonely game we play? Looking for the right words to say, searching but not finding, understanding anyway. We're lost in," what?

48. In Disney's "Mulan," what was the name of the leader of the Huns who wanted to take over all of China?

49. Richard Haydn's last movie role was in "Young Frankenstein" as Herr Falkstein, but he is most remembered as playing Uncle Max in what movie?

50. It's the debilitating disease that Margaret Shroeder's daughter contracts in the second season of the TV show "Boardwalk Empire."

Answers 41-50

41. Prince

42. Semet

43. Ryan Gosling

44. The Godfather

45. Coldplay

46. Comic Book Guy

47. This Masquerade

48. Shan-Yu

49. Sound of Music

50. Polio

Questions 51-60

51. Who released the song "A Perfect Sonnet" in 2000? This group was founded by singer-songwriter and guitarist Conor Oberst.

52. Morn was a minor character on what "Star Trek" spin-off?

53. In this 1949 British film noir a funeral is held for Harry Lime. Except, when police dig up his grave, some third person is in it. Name the film.

54. Who released the song "So Good" in 2012? This artist is the better known nickname of Bobby Ray Simmons, Jr.

55. "Well, it's one for the money, two for the show, three to get ready, now go, cat, go!" is the opening line of what song?

56. What cosmopolitan drink was reportedly invented in San Francisco in the 1800s?

57. This 1993 football drama was about a scrappy walk-on who was allowed to play in a Notre Dame game the final minutes of the last game of his college career.

58. Who released the song "Flashdance... What a Feeling" in 1983? This artist became famous for her role in the 1980 film "Fame" and her recording of the title song of the same name.

59. Inspired by Conan the Barbarian and Flash Gordon, which barbarian's 1980 cartoon is set in a future (A.D. 3994) post-apocalyptic wasteland divided into kingdoms mostly ruled by wizards?

60. What TV show used footage of the Family Truckster from "National Lampoon's Vacation" in its opening credits?

Answers 51-60

51. Bright Eyes

52. Deep Space Nine

53. The Third Man

54. B.o.B

55. Blue Suede Shoes

56. Martini

57. Rudy

58. Irene Cara

59. Thundarr

60. Married with Children

Questions 61-70

61. This was the name of the ship Indiana Jones booked to carry the Ark of the Covenant out of Egypt in "Raiders of the Lost Ark."

62. This 2007 film, which earned director Jason Reitman an Oscar for best screenplay, centered on a teenage girl's decision to give her baby to an unhappily married couple.

63. What ABC show did Peter Jennings interrupt to report that the Coca-Cola company was bringing back classic Coke after introducing New Coke only 3 months earlier?

64. If going by the year of theatrical release, who is the first Disney Princess?

65. In what 1970s TV show did Angie Dickinson play Pepper Anderson?

66. Who released the song "Club Michelle" in 1983? This artist handed out tickets as a police officer before he began belting out "Two Tickets to Paradise."

67. Which Seinfeld character gets into a fight with The Bubble Boy over an incorrectly-printed Trivial Pursuit card featuring the answer "The Moops?"

68. What is Bono's real name from the band U2?

69. Who sang about "D-I-V-O-R-C-E" in 1968? This song, and album of the same name, hit #1 on the Country charts for this artist.

70. What are the names of the best known marine mammal parks in the United States?

Answers 61-70

61. Bantu Wind

62. Juno

63. General Hospital

64. Snow White

65. Police Woman

66. Eddie Money

67. George

68. Paul David Hewson

69. Tammy Wynette

70. SeaWorld

Questions 71-80

71. What did flamboyant blues woman Memphis Minnie characteristically wear?

72. Who plays the most characters in "Monty Python and the Holy Grail?"

73. Marvel comic's Daredevil had the ability to determine the location of objects in the environment by use of reflected sound waves, whether generated by himself or ambient sound known as what power?

74. Who released the song "Barbados" in 1975? The duo of Geraint Wyn Hughes and Jeffrey Calvert was formed when they met through Hughes' band, Quasar.

75. Who released a sequel to his album "Thick as a Brick" 40 years after the original?

76. In 1983, what hard rock band appeared for the first time in public without their trademark makeup on MTV?

77. In Jim Davis' beloved comic strip "Garfield," what's the last name of Garfield's owner, John?

78. What ability encompasses invulnerability or partial invulnerability to all but specific events, or may simply be an inability to age normally?

79. It's the name of Mitchell and Cameron's adopted daughter on the TV show "Modern Family."

80. What's the nickname of the sitcom character who has been honored with a bronze statue in Milwaukee, WI?

Answers 71-80

71. Bracelet of Silver Dollars

72. Michael Palin

73. Echolocation

74. Typically Tropical

75. Jethro Tull

76. KISS

77. Arbuckle

79. Lily

80. Fonzie

Questions 81-90

81. Inspired by her filmmaking ex-husband, Madonna wrote and directed her first feature film, released in 2008 through "On Demand" cable, entitled what?

82. This railroad property, in the standard US version of Monopoly, is probably named for the streetcar that used to service Atlantic City, since no railroad by that name ever ran through the area.

83. In Disney's insanely popular High School Musical films, what is the name of the high school the signing students attend?

84. What is Roy Scheider's character's nickname in "The French Connection?"

85. Who released the song "Lullaby" in 2012? This Canadian musician performed the track "Everybody Knows," which was used in the 1990 film "Pump Up the Volume."

86. Name the 1998 comedy movie that this quote comes from, "I mean, say what you like about the tenets of National Socialism, dude, at least it's an ethos."

87. This cartoon character was designed to be the antithesis of SpongeBob SquarePants' optimistic and bubbly personality. He's cynical and unhappy, but isn't particularly threatening.

88. What NFL player was featured on the PAL version of the 1999 "Madden NFL" video game?

89. In what fictional Texas city was "The Best Little Whorehouse in Texas" located, according to the original play?

90. This Korean-American actor is well known for his role as Jin-Soo Kwon on the 2004-2010 TV series "Lost."

Answers 81-90

81. Filth & Wisdom

82. Short Line

83. East

84. Cloudy

85. Leonard Cohen

86. The Big Lebowski

87. Squidward

88. Garrison Hearst

89. Gilbert

90. Daniel Dae Kim

Questions 91-100

91. What political cartoonist hid his wife's nickname, Snooky, in most of his works?

92. What was the first Walt Disney animated classic released on videocassette?

93. Madonna starred as "Breathless" Mahoney in the film Dick Tracy (1990). Name the director, whom she dated briefly.

94. Who released the song "Trip the Darkness" in 2012? The members of this Italian metal band have nicknames like Pizza, Maus and Criz.

95. Paul McCartney sings, "Don't build your hopes to be let down. 'Cause I really feel it's time," then Michael Jackson sings, "I know she'll tell you I'm the one for her. 'Cause she said I blow her mind," in what Michael Jackson duet?

96. What "Weird Al" Yankovic album parodied Michael Jackson's "Bad" album?

97. "Many times I've been alone and many times I've cried. Anyway you'll never know the many ways I've tried," is from which Beatles song?

98. It's who Judah Rosenthal has supposedly killed in Woody Allen's 1989 film "Crimes and Misdemeanors."

99. Daniel Dae Kim plays Chin Ho Kelly in this police drama TV series that's re-imagines a 1968-1980 original series. Surf's up!

100. On what classic album cover does a Volkswagen with the license plate LMW 28IF famously appear?

Answers 91-100

91. George Fisher

92. Dumbo

93. Warren Beatty

94. Lacuna Coil

95. The Girl Is Mine

96. Even Worse

97. Long & Winding Road

98. Mistress

99. Hawaii Five-O

100. Abbey Road

Questions 101-110

101. What 1966 Beatles album's working title was reportedly "Abracadabra?"

102. Who released the song "Vision of Love" in 2012? This artist won the eighth season of "American Idol." The debut album, "Brand New Shoes," was actually released prior to the show.

103. This yellow-hatted, mustachioed menace was introduced in "Super Mario Land 2," and went on to star in several of his own spin-off games.

104. What was the title of Woody Allen's segment in the movie "New York Stories?"

105. In 2010, what movie was awarded a special Golden Raspberry Award for Worst Eye Gouging Use of 3D?

106. This 1997 comedy film starring Jim Carrey used the tagline, "Trust me."

107. "Now face north. Think about direction, wonder why you haven't before," is from which classic R.E.M. song?

108. Who released the song "Orpheo Looks Back" in 2012? Based on his name, he should be able to look back without moving his head to much.

109. What kills the Nazi monkey in "Raiders of the Lost Ark?"

110. Who released the song "All This Time" in 2012? She began singing at the age of 3 in her home church, Truth Temple of Kannapolis, North Carolina.

Answers 101-110

101. Revolver

102. Kris Allen

103. Wario

104. Oedipus Wrecks

105. The Last Airbender

106. Liar Liar

107. Stand

108. Andrew Bird

109. Poison Dates

110. Britt Nicole

Questions 111-120

111. What World War II Steven Spielberg film was Ben Stiller working on when he reportedly came up with the idea for his movie "Tropic Thunder"?

112. This TV family living at 1313 Mockingbird Lane often used "The Encyclopedia of Voodoo."

113. Hut! Hut! Hut! Hut! Hike! In the 1991 video game "Tecmo Super Bowl," which Oakland Raiders running back was nearly superhuman in speed?

114. Who released the song "Music" in 2000? This album, "Music," was critically praised for the artist's creativity and collaboration with Mirwais.

115. "Shook Me Like a Prayer," is a Rock Sugar mash-up of AC/DC's "Shook Me All Night Long" and Madonna's "Like a Prayer." What company paid Madonna $5 million for the rights to sponsor the world premiere of "Like a Prayer?"

116. Which "Dancing with the Stars" contestant began the Jive by crawling out of a doghouse?

117. What was the name of the volleyball in "Cast Away?"

118. Who wrote and starred as Mike in the 1996 film "Swingers?"

119. Who released the song "Be Alright" in 2012? At 12 years of age, this artist sang Ne-Yo's "So Sick" for a local singing competition and placed second.

120. Winona Ryder and Bridget Fonda both auditioned for the role of Amy Archer in The Hudsucker Proxy, but the part eventually went to what actress?

Answers 111-120

111. Empire of the Sun

112. The Munsters

113. Bo Jackson

114. Madonna

115. Pepsi Co.

116. Michael Bolton

117. Wilson

118. John Favreau

119. Justin Bieber

120. Jennifer Jason Leigh

Questions 121-130

121. Who released the song "I Fu**ed Up" in 2012? This song and "Gang Bang" are omitted from the Walmart edited deluxe edition of this artist's album.

122. Everyone knows that Sylvester Stallone played the title role in the "Rocky" movies, but what actress played Adrien? Yo, Adrien!

123. Which Broadway musical is responsible for the songs, "Anything You Can Do," "There's No Business Like Show Business," and "Doin' What Comes Naturally?"

124. What film did Francis Ford Coppola win a Best Writing award for at the 1971 Academy Awards?

125. What was the first musical play written by Rodgers and Hammerstein?

126. According to the Bee Gees, "Singin' them love songs. Singin' them straight to the heart songs. Blamin' it all on the," what?

127. This character was the first person to refer to Dr. Sloan as "McSteamy" on the TV show "Grey's Anatomy."

128. In Disney's "Sleeping Beauty," what's the name of Maleficent's pet raven who assists the evil fairy?

129. Who released the song "Breaking the Law" in 2012? She first became known after being featured on a single by rapper Chipmunk, "Diamond Rings."

130. Which abbreviation, used by Rachael Ray, was added to The Oxford American College Dictionary in 2007, with credit being given to her for coining the phrase?

Answers 121-130

121. Madonna

122. Talia Shire

123. Annie Get Your Gun

124. Patton

125. Oklahoma!

126. Nights on Broadway

127. Meredith Grey

128. Diablo

129. Emeli Sandé

130. EVOO

Questions 131-140

131. What film used the tagline, "They have a plan, but not a clue?"

132. A German businessman staffs his factory with Jews in order to protect them from the Nazis in what seven Oscar winning film, including Best Picture and Best Director?

133. Mr. Boddy has this colorful name in the original British version of "Cluedo."

134. Canadian musician Alannah Myles topped the charts with this song, crooning about "little boy's smiles" and "that slow Southern style," which is actually about the life of Elvis Presley.

135. What is the name of the cooking competition airing on the Food Network that pits chefs head to head in a timed competition with the winner receiving $10,000?

136. In which department store's window does Ralphie see the Red Rider BB gun at the beginning of "A Christmas Story?"

137. What is Rule #2 in "Zombieland," according to Columbus, that describes how to make sure a zombie is dead?

138. What charity organization did Rachael Ray launch with Bill Clinton to help children eat healthier?

139. "Wonder how you manage to make ends meet. Who finds the money when you pay the rent? Did you think that money was heaven sent?" is from which Beatles song?

140. Which Broadway musical was based on the book by Christopher Isherwood and is set in 1931 Berlin as the Nazi's are rising to power?

Answers 131-140

131. O Brother, Where Art Thou?

132. Schindler's List

133. Dr. Black

134. Black Velvet

135. Challenge

136. Higbee's

137. Double Tap

138. The Yum-o! Organization

139. Lady Madonna

140. Cabaret

Questions 141-150

141. What is Marion's last name in "Raiders of the Lost Ark?"

142. What is the first word in the Beatles' song "Lucy in the Sky with Diamonds?"

143. What actress, at her begging, is the only singer to be dubbed in Woody Allen's musical "Everyone Says I Love You?"

144. What actor, paraphrased a line from Spider-Man, "With great power comes great responsibility, in The Coens' "The Ladykillers?"

145. "I met a gin soaked barroom queen in Memphis. She tried to take me upstairs for a ride. She had to heave me right across her shoulder. Cause I just can't seem to drink you off my mind," is from which Rolling Stones classic song?

146. What does Alfred Hitchcock miss in his cameo in "North By Northwest?"

147. Who released the song "Breakfast" in 2012? This group consists of Chidera Anamege and Noah Beresin.

148. What film used the tagline, "Crushed lips don't talk." This 1953 drama was directed by Alfred Hitchcock and based on a 1902 play by Paul Anthelme called "Nos Deux Consciences."

149. She is the reason all stepmothers have an uphill battle, but her name wasn't "The Wicked Stepmother." What was her actual name in Disney's "Cinderella"?

150. What film used the tagline, "Fear is a place?"

Answers 141-150

141. Ravenwood

142. Picture

143. Drew Barrymore

144. J.K. Simmons

145. Honky Tonk Women

146. Bus

147. Chiddy Bang

148. I Confess

149. Lady Tremaine

150. Session 9

Questions 151-160

151. This 1991 presidential film used the tagline, "The story that won't go away."

152. "Steppin' Out With My Baby" rejuvenated what crooner's career in 1993?

153. Which Broadway musical is a juke box musical based on the music of the "Four Seasons?"

154. In 2010, "The Last Airbender" was the first PG-13 or lower rated movie that M. Night Shyamalan had directed since his directorial debut, which was what 1998 film starring Denis Leary and Rosie O'Donnell?

155. What disabilitating disease does Margaret Shroeder's daughter contract in the second season of "Boardwalk Empire"?

156. In February 2010, MTV officially dropped what two-word phrase from its original tagline, effectively neutering the station's acronym?

157. On what movie set did Steven Spielberg cover Alfred Molina in taratulas for his first scene on his first day of filming?

158. Who released the song "Anthem" in 1975? This ageless 3-man band is comprised of Geddy Lee, Alex Lifeson and Neil Peart.

159. Created in 1984, which cartoon series featured a group of 12 (and later, 14) pre-adolescent anthropomorphic animal characters in the fictional town of Green Meadow, who had a club that met in an abandoned caboose?

160. Who released the song "I'm Not In Love" in 1975? This English band initially consisted of Lol Creme, Kevin Godley, Graham Gouldman and Eric Stewart.

Answers 151-160

151. JFK

152. Tony Bennett

153. Jersey Boys

154. Wide Awake

155. Polio

156. Music Television

157. Raiders of the Lost Ark

158. Rush

159. The Get Along Gang

160. 10cc

Questions 161-170

161. Who released the song "How We Do (Party)" in 2012? This British singer-songwriter appeared on BBC's "Eurovision: Your Country Needs You" in 2009.

162. What website promotes the official "Star Wars" fan film awards?

163. Who released the song "Country Boys Like Me" in 2012? Matt Bjorke of "Roughstock" said of this country music album, "[He] has certainly returned with a strong album worthy of becoming a collection of big hits."

164. What "Brady Bunch" child actor was the subject of reality shows? He was also a game show host.

165. In The Omen II, what character believed to be the Antichrist, is protected by evil creatures that kill those who would stop him?

166. What Brian Michael Bendis comic book features the character Christian Walker?

167. Jimmy Darmody is a veteran of what war in the HBO series "Boardwak Empire"?

168. It's the year Marty McFly returned to in "Back to the Future Part III." It was the same year Cleveland succeeded Arthur as the 22nd U.S. president.

169. What fictional Illinois town does John Hughes set a majority of his films in?

170. Which Broadway play saw Matthew Broderick win a Tony Award for "Best Actor in a Play" in 1983?

Answers 161-170

161. Rita Ora

162. AtomFilms.com

163. Craig Morgan

164. Christopher Knight

165. Damien Thorn

166. Powers

167. WWI

168. 1885

169. Shermer

170. Brighton Beach Memoirs

Questions 171-180

171. Who released the song "Unknown" in 2000? Jason Wade, lead singer and songwriter of this band, originally formed it as a church rock band.

172. Who released the song "Do My Thing" in 2012? This artist is an English Grammy Award winning R&B singer-songwriter, rapper and record producer.

173. Despite being a prolific lyricist, bluesman John Lee Hooker could not do what?

174. The eighth (and last) season of this show, which was the most-watched comedy series internationally in 2010, began on September 25th, 2011, with the secret burial of an evil stepfather in the woods off Wisteria Lane.

175. Who was the lead singer for The Supremes in the 1960s?

176. What composers operas include "The Barber of Seville" and "William Tell?"

177. Which Broadway musical saw its film adaptation take home an Academy Award for Best Picture in 1984?

178. This character on "All in the Family" would sometimes complain about newsman Walter Cronkite, calling him "Pinko Cronkite."

179. Who released the song "The Refugee" in 1983? It was found on their third studio album, "War."

180. What Audioslave album title track was featured on the "Madden NFL '07" video game soundtrack?

Answers 171-180

171. Lifehouse

172. Estelle

173. Read or Write

174. Desperate Housewives

175. Diana Ross

176. Gioacchino Rossini

177. Amadeus

178. Archie Bunker

179. U2

180. Revelations

Questions 181-190

181. What rap group is known for the song "Insane in the Membrane?"

182. It's the first and last name of the actress who took her first name from Shakespeare's "The Merchant of Venice." She's best known for her roles on "Ally McBeal" and "Arrested Development."

183. Who was nominated for an Oscar for portraying Tina Turner in "What's Love Got To Do With It?" a 2002 film that tracked the relationship of Ike and Tina Turner.

184. In the 1985 film "Weird Science," what's the name of the fantasy woman that Wyatt and Gary create using their computer, played by Kelly LeBrock?

185. This "Star Wars" movie was promoted on Virgin Atlantic with printed airsickness bags featuring important information such as "Lightsaber Etiquette" and "Seating Jedi and Sith."

186. "And when the groove is dead and gone. You know that love survives, so we can rock forever" is the end of what Michael Jackson song?

187. Gene Wilder and Mel Brooks received Best Adapted Screenplay nominations at the 1975 Oscars for Young Frankenstein. However, they lost to the writers of what other film?

188. What 1980s cartoon series is about an animatronic teddy bear who leaves his home on the island of Rillonia with his best friend Grubby to follow an ancient map?

189. What European city is the setting for Woody Allen's "Match Point?"

190. Who says office romances never work? Warren Beatty married this "Bugsy" co-star.

Answers 181-190

181. Cypress Hill

182. Portia De Rossi

183. Angela Bassett

184. Lisa

185. Revenge of the Sith

186. Rock With You

187. Godfather Part II

188. Teddy Ruxpin

189. London

190. Annette Bening

Questions 191-200

191. Who was the first singer to appear in the opening credits of a James Bond film?

192. This director of the 1980 film "Used Cars" also directed 1985's "Back to the Future."

193. She played Detective Anita Van Buren on the TV show "Law & Order."

194. Which Broadway musical, first performed in 1943, won a special Tony Award for its 50th anniversary in 1993?

195. This actress played Sandy in the movie version of the Broadway musical "Grease."

196. What singer's 1992 debut album was "What's the 411?"

197. Which balance-based board game gets its name from the imperative form of the Swahili verb "to build?"

198. "They're out to get you, better leave while you can. Don't wanna be a boy, you wanna be a man. You wanna stay alive, better do what you can," is from what Michael Jackson song?

199. What is Norm's real first name on the NBC sitcom "Cheers"?

200. Who convinced her parents to let her move to L.A. to pursue acting with a powerpoint presentation titled: "Project Hollywood"?

Answers 191-200

191. Sheena Easton

192. Robert Zemeckis

193. S. Epatha Merkerson

194. Oklahoma

195. Olivia Newton-John

196. Mary J. Blige

197. Jenga

198. Beat It

199. Hillary

200. Emma Stone

Questions 201-210

201. Who released the song "Taste in Men" in 2000? This British alternative rock band was formed in London in 1994 by singer-guitarist Brian Molko and guitarist/bassist Stefan Olsdal.

202. Who released the song "We Take Care of Our Own" in 2012? Not shy nor unseen before, this opening track reflects the artist's frustration with the lack of accountability he sees in government.

203. Which Broadway musical was first performed on Broadway with Tim Curry playing the role of Mozart and Jane Seymour playing his wife, Constanze?

204. What's the title of the Baby Herman cartoon in "Who Framed Roger Rabbit?"

205. What was George Jefferson's English neighbor's name on the TV show "The Jeffersons," who occasionally needed George to walk on his back?

206. Bob Marley & The Wailers asked someone to, "Come rub on my belly," like this tropical fruit preserve in a song that was later covered by Barbra Streisand.

207. What outspoken first lady and icon for women's rights, who passed away in 2011, founded a center for substance abuse and addiction in 1982, and received the Congressional Gold Medal in 1988?

208. "Once you get rid of integrity, the rest is a piece of cake," is a famous line from what TV character?

209. Prince and the Revolution sang about a girl wearing this fruit-colored beret. It was "the kind you find in a secondhand store."

210. What character is hosting a party in the film "Superbad" that Seth desperately wants to attend?

Answers 201-210

201. Placebo

202. Bruce Springsteen

203. Amadeus

204. What's Cooking

205. Harry Bentley

206. Guava Jelly

207. Betty Ford

208. J.R. Ewing

209. Raspberry

210. Jules

Questions 211-220

211. Who was the second Spanish-born actor to win an Oscar after her husband became the first?

212. What type of car was the General Lee in the TV show "Dukes of Hazzard"?

213. What collaborative album won Album of the Year at the 51st Grammy awards in 2009?

214. Who released the song "Land of Hope and Dreams" in 2012? The song was actually written sometime in the late-90s and first performed on the 1999 Reunion Tour with the E Street Band.

215. Which illness was Paula Deen diagnosed with that caused many former fans to call her a hypocrite for promoting her high carb, high fat recipes?

216. Who released the song "These Times" in 2012? This band from Tulsa, OK, was originally named Crew, but changed their name after signing with Universal Records.

217. Who released the song "If I Never Met You" in 1999? This artist has won an Oscar, Emmy, Grammy and Tony Award.

218. Who released the song "Somethin' 'Bout a Truck" in 2012? This song was the first single from the debut album, "Up All Night," for this country music singer.

219. What legendary banjo picker got a star on the "Hollywood Walk of Fame" in 2003?

220. In this Ian Fleming novel & James Bond film, Kronsteen, the main villain, is a chess master and main strategist for SPECTRE.

Answers 211-220

211. Penelope Cruz

212. Dodge Charger

213. Raising Sand

214. Bruce Springsteen

215. Type II Diabetes

216. SafetySuit

217. Barbra Streisand

218. Kip Moore

219. Earl Scruggs

220. From Russia With Love

Questions 221-231

221. Which long running Broadway musical has actors and actresses singing songs such as "Seventy-six Trombones" and "Shipoopi?"

222. Who released the song "Lazy Projector" in 2012? This artist's early jazz influences were Johnny Hodges, Lester Young and Fats Waller.

223. Making her debut on March 9, 1959, this icon's full name is Barbara Millicent Roberts. Name this popular character.

224. Who sang the lines "Trailers for sale or rent. Rooms to let: 50 cents?"

225. Name the middle school that's home to The 25th Annual Putnam County Spelling Bee according to the Broadway musical of the same name.

226. What experimental Lennon song did Paul McCartney, Ringo Starr and George Harrison try to keep off the Beatles' "White Album"?

227. What is Sue's middle name on the ABC show "The Middle?"

228. What 1982 science fiction film directed by Ridley Scott used the tagline, "Man has made his match... now it's his problem."

229. What was the occupation of the person that Hannibal Lector enjoyed with some fava beans and a nice Chianti?

230. Who plays the role of Queen Amidala in the "Star Wars" Episodes I and II movies?

Answers 221-230

221. Music Man

222. Andrew Bird

223. Barbie

224. Roger Miller

225. Putnam Valley

226. Revolution 9

227. Sue

228. Blade Runner

229. Census Taker

230. Natalie Portman

Questions 231-240

231. What band was recording "The Piper at the Gates of Dawn" at Abbey Road Studios while the Beatles were recording "Sgt. Pepper's Lonely Hearts Club Band"?

232. Who played Buffy the Vampire Slayer in the original film of the same name?

233. What comic strip's characters include a talking cigarette named Mr. Butts?

234. Who released the song "Black Rock" in 2000? In 2005, the single "Love and Memories" became the first by this band to receive significant radio airplay.

235. He's the host of The Discovery Channel's TV show "Dirty Jobs."

236. Which lingerie company was Jane Russell a spokeswoman for in the 1970s?

237. What movie's Hungarian title is "Give Your Life Expensive?"

238. "I'd spend a lifetime waiting for the right time. Now that your near the time is here at last," is from what Elvis song?

239. What popular game show producer created a television version of Monopoly which ran during the summer of 1990 and featured Mike Reilly as the host?

240. Leopold and Loeb were the inspiration for what Hitchcock film with a one-word title?

Answers 231-240

231. Pink Floyd

232. Kristy Swanson

233. Doonesbury

234. O.A.R.

235. Mike Rowe

236. Playtex

237. Die Hard

238. It's Now Or Never

239. Merv Griffin

240. Rope

Questions 241-250

241. Challenging product stakeholders to give the demonstration of their lives, this king of the ring event is a favorite of International Consumer Electronics Show attendees.

242. Who released the song "Runaway Train" in 1992? This artist was born Reginald Kenneth Dwight on March 25, 1947.

243. What "Silkwood" star's parents married and divorced each other 3 times?

244. Who released the song "Naked" in 2012? She was discovered after her friend Shane Crislip posted her singing to some beats on Myspace.

245. In this hit, the Bee Gees sang, "Tried to hitch a ride to San Francisco, gotta do the things I wanna do. And the lights all went out in" where?

246. In the 1994 film "The Mask," Jim Carrey plays Stanley Ipkiss who works in what banking job?

247. Who released the song "Out 2 Space" in 2012? In 2009, the popular Myspace profile "Pretty Much Amazing" featured 5 songs by this band.

248. Who released the song "La Grande" in 2012? This artist toured as the opening act for Colin Meloy, lead singer of The Decemberists, in 2008.

249. Who released the song "Babylon" in 2000? This English singer-songwriter released his first album in 1993, but didn't receive worldwide until six years later with the release of his 1998 album "White Ladder."

250. In "The Muppet Movie," this actor plays the villainous Doc Hopper, who wants Kermit to star in the commercials for his Frog Leg restaurant.

Answers 241-250

241. Last Gadget Standing

242. Elton John

243. Cher

244. Dev

245. Massachusetts

246. Clerk

247. Chiddy Bang

248. Laura Gibson

249. David Gray

250. Charles Durning

Questions 251-260

251. What was the name of Frasier's kick-ass, star-making agent on the NBC sitcom "Fraiser"?

252. Bob Dylan wrote this song featuring the lyrics, "She was married when we first met, soon to be divorced, I helped her out of a jam, I guess, but I used a little too much force."

253. In the fifth incarnation of the Scooby-Doo cartoon series, The Scooby-Doo & Scrappy-Doo/Puppy Hour (1982-1983), the audience is introduced to Scooby-Doo's more courageous brother, a white Great Dane named what?

254. "Don't Stop the Sandman," is a mash-up between Metalica's "Enter Sandman" and "Don't Stop Believin'" by what San Francisco rock band comprised of former members of Santana?

255. What part is given to Olive in David Shayne's drama in Woody Allen's "Bullets Over Broadway" because she's dating the mobster financing the play?

256. "I don't want to leave her now, you know I believe and how," ends every verse of what Beatles song?

257. Reverend Shaw Moore wants to outlaw dancing in his small town, but newcomer Ren McCormick has other plans. Eventually, prom takes place at this high school in the movie "Footloose."

258. Who released the song "Love Rollercoaster" in 1975? This group is also well known for their 1970s hit "Fire."

259. What film did "Deliverance" lose to for Best Picture in 1973?

260. Which 1960s cartoon featured an ape dressed in human accessories with a small hat and a bow tie? It featured the recurring characters Punkin' Puss, Mushmouse, Ricochet Rabbit and Droop-a-Long.

Answers 251-260

251. Bebe

252. Tangled Up in Blue

253. Yabba-Doo

254. Journey

255. The Psychiatrist

256. Something

257. Beaumont

258. The Ohio Players

259. The Godfather

260. Magilla Gorilla

Questions 261-270

261. The criminals of Hamsterdam and the law trying to fight them on TV's "The Wire" are located in what East Coast town?

262. According to Alan Alda's character, Lester, in "Crimes and Misdemeanors", what is comedy?

263. What is the name of the priest mentioned in The Beatles song "Eleanor Rigby?"

264. Which chef was referred to by the female chefs as "Hollywood" on Season 9 of "Top Chef?"

265. What fitness guru was born in New Orleans in 1948?

266. What film used the tagline, "You don't assign him to murder cases. You just turn him loose?"

267. What young actress plays Isabelle in the Marty Scorcese film "Hugo?"

268. "Sitting here wasted and wounded at this old piano. Trying hard to capture the moment this morning I don't know. 'Cause a bottle of vodka is still lodged in my head," is from which Bon Jovi song?

269. Who released the song "Vereda Tropical" in 1983? At Woodstock in 1969, this band was recognized for their Latin sound, which was much different from the rest of the line up at the show.

270. This actress, winner of numerous Emmy Awards, most recently won in 2010 for Outstanding Guest actress in a comedy series. She received her first Emmy nomination in 1951. Who is she?

Answers 261-270

261. Baltimore

262. Tragedy plus time.

263. Father McKenzie

264. Chris Crary

265. Richard Simmons

266. Dirty Harry

267. Chloe Grace Moretz

268. Bed of Roses

269. Santana

270. Betty White

Questions 271-280

271. What English pioneering rock band led by Ozzy released the song "Supertzar" in 1975?

272. What is the name of the South American Indian tribe that chases Indiana Jones through the jungle at the beginning of "Raiders of the Lost Ark?"

273. This character on "Arrested Development" suffers from "never-nude" syndrome, which is the desire to avoid anyone (including himself) seeing his genitalia.

274. What film used the tagline, "Catch it?"

275. A contest was held in 2003 to add a new ailment to Cavity Sam in the game of Operation & this ice cream cone head injury was added in 2004.

276. What couple is said to have had the longest lasting Hollywood marriage at 69 years?

277. What alternative rock star had a smash hit with "Lullaby" on his 2008 album "Honeydew."

278. This popular character actor, who played The Wizard in "Taxi Driver," had John Lennon as his best man at his wedding.

279. How many people are seen killed in "Kill Bill: Volume 2?"

280. This 1995 western film starring Russell Crowe, Leonardo DiCaprio, Gene Hackman and Sharon Stone used the tagline, "Think you're quick enough."

Answers 271-280

271. Black Sabbath

272. Hovitos

273. Tobias Funke

274. Saturday Night Fever

275. Brain Freeze

276. Bob & Delores Hope

277. Shawn Mullins

278. Peter Boyle

279. 3

280. The Quick & the Dead

Questions 281-290

281. What actor had a voice cameo as a cursed actor in "Rosemary's Baby?"

282. Who won the Oscar for Best Actress for her performance in the film "The Lion in Winter?"

283. What soap opera comic strip sees advice distributed by a 60-year-old widow?

284. Who released the song "Sara Smile" in 1975? This duo was best known for their hit singles "Rich Girl", "Kiss on My List" and "Maneater."

285. What film used the tagline, "A man went looking for America and couldn't find it?"

286. "Close your eyes and I'll kiss you, tomorrow I'll miss you. Remember I'll always be true," is from which Beatles love song?

287. What film used the tagline, "Suddenly, life was more than French fries, gravy, and girls?"

288. It's Pierce Brosnan's name in the 2005 dark comedy, "The Matador."

289. Who was nominated for a Razzy in 1980 for directing "The Shining?"

290. This film used the tagline, "Good Girls Want Him Bad. Bad Girls Want Him Worse."

Answers 281-290

281. Tony Curtis

282. Katharine Hepburn

283. Mary Worth

284. Hall & Oates

285. Easy Rider

286. All My Loving

287. Diner

288. Julian Noble

289. Stanley Kubrick

290. Cry-Baby

Questions 291-300

291. In "Casino Royale," in what card game does Le Chiffe have great expertise?

292. Who's the only actor to receive an Oscar nomination for a performance in any of the "Star Wars" movies? He received the nomination in 1977 for Best Supporting Actor.

293. Who released the song "I Don't Give A" in 2012? Prior to this album, the artist posted this message on her Facebook page, "I'm on the lookout for the maddest, sickest, most badass people to collaborate with."

294. What film used the tagline, "She brought a small town to its feet and a huge corporation to its knees?"

295. Who released the song "Countdown To Extinction" in 1992? The album of the same name was the most successful of all the albums produced by this American heavy metal band.

296. In the 1984 film "Ghostbusters," outside of what building does Dr. Peter Venkman run into Dana Barrett? It's also where she plays the cello.

297. Almost every line of what Beatles song is repeated, "Got a good reason, for taking the easy way out. Got a good reason, for taking the easy way out, now?"

298. Which "Top Chef" Season 5 runner-up and "Top Chef: All-stars" contestant earned a job on "The Chew?"

299. This 2004 film directed by Mel Gibson covers the final 12 hours of Jesus' life, beginning with the Agony in the Garden and ending with his resurrection.

300. What 1980's television sitcom features the characters Elyse Keaton and Alex P. Keaton?

Answers 291-300

291. Texas Hold 'Em

292. Alec Guinness

293. Madonna

294. Erin Brockovich

295. Megadeth

296. Carnegie Hall

297. Day Tripper

298. Carla Hall

299. Passion of the Christ

300. Family Ties

Questions 301-310

301. "They call me Mister Tibbs!" was such an awesome quote it became the title of the sequel to what 1960s film?

302. What was the original title for "Butch Cassidy and the Sundance Kid?"

303. Who released the song "Rock DJ" in 2000? This artist launched his solo career after many disagreements with the pop group Take That, which rose to fame in the early-90s.

304. What panned Beatles movie wasn't shown in the U.S. until 1976?

305. What's the name of the classic children's story by Anna Sewell that features a 6-year-old horse? It has spawned many movies of the same name.

306. Seattle rockers The Presidents of the United States of America scored a Grammy nomination for this song about a man moving to the country to eat him a lot of what?

307. Who was the lead vocalist for AC/DC from 1974 to 1980?

308. What Charles Mingus jazz master work takes 2 hours to perform?

309. Who released the song "Forever" in 2012? He's the lead vocalist, rhythm guitarist and founding member of the rock group, Staind.

310. He's the character played by Stanely Tucci in the 2010 teen comedy film "Easy A."

Answers 301-310

301. In the Heat of the Night

302. The Sundance Kid & Butch Cassidy

303. Robbie Williams

304. Magical Mystery Tour

305. Black Beauty

306. Peaches

307. Bon Scott

308. Epitaph

309. Aaron Lewis

310. Dill Penderghast

Questions 311-320

311. This famous Kansas Citian was born Lucille Fay LeSueur, but became an actress in film, television and theater under an entirely different name.

312. Who released the song "White Lines" in 1983? This artist is a DJ and mixing icon.

313. Who released the song "Lifetime" in 2012? She released her first solo single "Heaven" in August 2011.

314. Dueling Banjos famously opened this Burt Reynolds and Ned Beatty film about a river-rafting expedition gone horribly wrong.

315. Whose song "Runaway" was used for the theme of TV's "Crime Story?"

316. This "Law & Order: SVU" character was also on the first three seasons of the TV show "Law & Order."

317. What year did "Out of Africa" beat "The Color Purple" and "Witness" to win Best Picture? The World Cup was played in Mexico in the same year.

318. This supervillain, played by Liam Neeson in the film "Batman Begins," often refers to the caped crusader as "Detective."

319. What country band took its name from a phone number on a "Hee-Haw" sketch?

320. What's Rule Number 8 in the film "Zombieland" according to Jesse Eisenberg's character, Columbus?

Answers 311-320

311. Joan Crawford

312. Grandmaster Flash

313. Emeli Sandé

314. Deliverance

315. Del Shannon

316. Dann Florek

317. 1986

318. Ra's al Ghul

319. BR5-49

320. Get a Kickass Partner

Questions 321-330

321. What is Manny terrified of on the TV show "Modern Family?"

322. What boxer named all five of his sons, and a grill, after himself?

323. Who released the song "Happy Phantom" in 1992?

324. Which actress hoarsely explained, "I want to be alone," in 1932's "Grand Hotel?"

325. This 1999 teen romantic comedy was a contemporary take on Shakespeare's "The Taming of the Shrew." It also spawned a 2008 TV series.

326. Who released the song "Sleeping Beauty" in 2000? This band was formed when Tool's Maynard Keenan allowed guitarist Billy Howerdel to stay in his North Hollywood home.

327. Who released the song "Better Off Alone" in 1999? It sounds like a female artist, but it's actually a Dutch eurodance group.

328. This public radio program bills itself as, "The Oddly Informative News Quiz."

329. Who released the song "King Of Pain" in 1983?

330. What repeated name is the title of a Woody Allen film staring Will Ferrell as Hobie?

Answers 321-330

321. Butterflies

322. George Foreman

323. Tori Amos

324. Greta Garbo

325. 10 Things I Hate About You

326. A Perfect Circle

327. Alice Deejay

328. Wait Wait... Don't Tell Me

329. The Police

330. Melinda and Melinda

Questions 331-340

331. Who released the song "Bunny Rabbits Are Nice" in 1992?

332. What film used the tagline, "Not every gift is a blessing?"

333. Who released the song "Sweating Bullets" in 1992? Dave Mustaine said about this song, "I wrote that about myself. It was pointed out to me that I'm kind of schizophrenic and that I live inside my head."

334. Who released the song "Part of Me" in 2012? This song is the lead single from the artist's 2012 re-release of her second album, "Teenage Dream," in 2010.

335. Bobby Drake, of the original X-Men, was more commonly known as this because of his cryokinetic ability to freeze.

336. Who released the song "Bad Blood" in 1975?

337. To whom does Margaret Schroeder sign over Nucky's undeveloped land to at the end of "Boardwalk Empire" season 2?

338. Who said, "Start every day with a smile and get it over with?"

339. What film used the tagline, "Bigger. Smarter. Faster. Meaner?"

340. What type of car was the General Lee in the TV show "Dukes of Hazzard?"

Answers 331-340

331. Kimberly Perry

332. The Sixth Sense

333. Megadeth

334. Katy Perry

335. Iceman

336. Neil Sedaka

337. Catholic Church

338. W.C. Fields

339. Deep Blue Sea

340. Dodge Charger

Questions 341-350

341. This 1987 romantic comedy, nominated for six Oscars, stars, among others, Nicolas Cage as a man who lost his hand in a bread slicer.

342. In what year does the movie "The Green Mile" begin?

343. What 1977 animated film's home video release was recalled by Disney due to some objectionable background images of naked women?

344. Who released the song "No Future" in 2012? During a 5-month break from The Hold Steady, this artist recorded this track on his solo album, "Clear Heart Full Eyes."

345. "Young Frankenstein" wasn't the only film Gene Wilder, Marty Feldman and Madeline Kahn starred in together. The other film has which famous detective in the title?

346. Who released the song "Mr. Roboto" in 1983? On this rock operatic album, Kilroy escapes using the Mr. Roboto disguise. Long live rock 'n' roll!

347. Who played "Marcus Welby M.D.?"

348. Which two characters on the TV show "Law & Order" are recovering alcoholics?

349. What was the original title of the film "The Blob?"

350. Who released the song "Californication" in 1999?

Answers 341-350

341. Moonstruck

342. 1935

343. The Rescuers

344. Craig Finn

345. Sherlock Holmes

346. Styx

347. Robert Young

348. Briscoe & Cragen

349. The Glob

350. Red Hot Chili Peppers

Questions 351-360

351. For the Oscar winning movie, "No Country For Old Men," there was only one actor in the cast who had worked with the Coen Brothers previously. Name this actor, perhaps most famous for his role in "Newsradio."

352. Who released the song "Sunday Morning Call" in 2000? This song provided the first time that Noel sang lead vocals over his brother Liam on an A-side since 1996's "Don't Look Back in Anger."

353. Which 1971 protest song was written by and about Johnny Cash as an explanation for the nickname on his stage appearance and style of dress?

354. He's married to the often-mentioned but never-seen Vera on the TV sitcom "Cheers."

355. Tori Amos released this concept album, featuring the singles "Taxi Ride" and "A Sorta Fairytale," which tells the tale of a young girl's cross country travels from Los Angeles to New York.

356. "Sarcastic mister know it all. Close your eyes and I'll kiss you 'cause. With the birds I'll share, with the birds I'll share," are lyrics from which Red Hot Chili Peppers song?

357. Who released the song "Tell Her About It" in 1983? This song from the album "An Innocent Man" attempts to convince a young man to tell a woman how he feels about her before he misses his chance.

358. American composer Philip Glass' works are described as what?

359. Which character on the TV sitcom "Will & Grace" did Dr. Leo Markus marry? The good doctor was played by Harry Connick, Jr.

360. On the TV show "Arrested Development," whose girlfriend does Michael Bluth accidentally call "bland."

Answers 351-360

351. Stephen Root

352. Oasis

353. Man in Black

354. Norm

355. Scarlet's Walk

356. Scar Tissue

357. Billy Joel

358. Minimalist

359. Grace

360. George Michael

Questions 361-370

361. What George Gershwin song was Al Capone's favorite tune?

362. What banner year for Steven Spielberg saw the debut of "Schindler's List" and "Jurassic Park?"

363. The POTUS is a popular character referenced on The West Wing. But who is the FLOTUS?

364. This 2008 Oscar winning documentary, directed by James Marsh, chronicles Philippe Petit's 1974 high-wire walk between the Twin Towers of New York's World Trade Center.

365. Which Broadway musical is based on the music of the 1980s, and features bands like Styx, Journey, Bon Jovi and Twisted Sister?

366. "Ok, you want plain English: Robin is gonna be dead. D-E-D. Dead," is a line spoken by what actor in "Robin Hood: Men in Tights" (1993)?

367. What home business owned by Paula Deen did she quickly outgrow before she was forced to open a restaurant to stay in business?

368. Who released the song "Nothing to Gein" in 2000? This song on the album "L.D. 50" was inspired by a 1950s murderer and body snatcher from Plainfield, WI.

369. In the U.S. edition of "Monopoly: Here and Now," you can now purchase what famous theme park for $2.4 million?

370. "I read bad poetry into your machine. I save your messages just to hear your voice. You always listen carefully to awkward rhymes. You always say your name, like I wouldn't know it's you," is from which R.E.M. song?

Answers 361-370

361. Rhapsody in Blue

362. 1993

363. First Lady of the United States

364. Man on Wire

365. Rock Of Ages

366. Dom DeLuise

367. The Bag Lady

368. Mudvayne

369. Walt Disney World

370. At My Most Beautiful

Questions 371-380

371. The television series Glee features singers from the glee club of what fictional high school, named after a president, located in Lima, Ohio?

372. DC Comic's Doctor Polaris and X-Men's Magneto could manipulate metal because they had the ability to control and generate what?

373. Professor Toru Tanaka played this menacing gladiator with a razor-bladed hockey stick who hunted Arnold Schwarzenegger in the 1987 film "The Running Man."

374. Who released the song "The Crying Game" in 1992?

375. "Breaking the Love," is a Rock Sugar mash-up of "Breaking the Law" by Judas Priest and "I'm Not in Love" by what English art-rock band popular during the 1970s?

376. He pitched for the Boston Red Sox before buying a bar on the TV show "Cheers."

377. Who released the song "Rhinestone Cowboy" in 1975?

378. What Disney "documentary" staged a scene of lemmings commiting mass suicide?

379. "Jesus died for somebody's sins but not mine," is from which Patti Smith song?

380. This long-running U.S. soap opera ended with a story about the cancellation of a fictional soap opera called "Fraternity Row."

Answers 371-380

371. McKinley

372. Magnetic Fields

373. Sub-Zero

374. Boy George

375. 10cc

376. Sam Malone

377. Glen Campbell

378. White Wilderness

379. Gloria

380. One Life to Live

Questions 381-390

381. What word did heats, rice, moss, ties, needs, lens, ice, nurse, leaks and meats almost rhyme with on David Letterman's very first Top Ten?

382. What Xbox game was the only game launched before the console was released?

383. What software company developed the game "Aces Over Europe?"

384. Which Broadway musical about a struggle for redemption and resolution ran from 1987 until 2003, and won Best Musical at the Tony Awards in 1987?

385. Who released the song "Goin' Down" in 2000? This song is a track from the band's debut album that was dropped in favor of "Whatever" for the major-label release.

386. "Don't you know I feel the same, 'cause nothin' lasts forever. And we both know hearts can change, and it's hard to hold a candle," in the what?

387. What HBO standup comedy program was created by music mogul Russell Simmons and hosted by Martin Lawrence when it debuted?

388. What 1989 Bonnie Raitt album won three Grammy Awards?

389. Who released the song "Big Boys Bickering" in 1992?

390. What DC Comics superhero has a power ring that must be recharged every 24 hours?

Answers 381-390

381. Peas

382. 4x4 EVO 2

383. Sierra

384. Les Miserables

385. Godsmack

386. Cold November Rain

387. Def Comedy Jam

388. Nick of Time

389. Paul McCartney

390. Green Lantern

Questions 391-400

391. Who released the song "I Won't Give Up" in 2012? This artist gained popularity with the single "The Remedy (I Won't Worry)," but it wasn't until 2005's album "Mr. A-Z" that larger success was achieved.

392. Which movie fighter had a wife named Adrian?

393. What Josh Hartnett war movie recreates the events of an army helicopter crash in Somalia based on the events related in the Mark Bowden novel of the same name?

394. Including all utilities and railroads, how many properties total are there available for purchase on a standard US Monopoly board?

395. This member of the Monty Python troupe performed The Lumberjack Song during a famous sketch from Monty Python's Flying Circus, where he sings about chopping down trees, wearing high heels, suspenders and a bra.

396. Which 1986-1987 cartoon characters, based on a toy of the same name, resemble colorful teddy bears or rabbits with long, pompom-tipped tails, have pouches on their backs that can be everted so they resemble fuzzy balls?

397. Based on a Jack London novel, what 1991 film features a gold miner and the dog he saves from a cruel owner?

398. How many "E" tiles are included in a game of Scrabble?

399. The radio character Yukon King was this type of dog in the radio and TV versions of "Challenge of the Yukon."

400. What film used the tagline, "Wanna date?"

Answers 391-400

391. Jason Mraz

392. Rocky

393. Black Hawk Down

394. 28

395. Michael Palin

396. Popples

397. White Fang

398. 12

399. Alaskan Husky

400. Frankenhooker

Questions 401-410

401. DC Comic's Phantom Girl (or Apparition) and X-Men's Kitty Pride could phase through solid matter without harm known as what?

402. This life-size sculpture is loved by its owner Jay Pritchett, but hated by his wife, Gloria, on the TV show "Modern Family."

403. Who released the song "Jack The Ripper" in 1992?

404. This actor has won five Emmy Awards, four for portraying a lawyer in a comedy series and one for portraying a defendant in a lawyer drama.

405. What Lennon-composed Beatles song was originally intended as a campaign song for Timothy Leary?

406. What actor starred in both "Jaws" and "Close Encounters of the Third Kind" for Steven Spielberg?

407. What is the nickname of the eighteen-month period in which John Lennon separated from Yoko Ono?

408. Who released the song "Slow Ride" in 1975?

409. "I'm gettin' bugged driving up and down the same old strip. I gotta find a new place where the kids are hip," is from what Beach Boys song?

410. This dance is the slowest Latin dance performed on "Dancing with the Stars."

Answers 401-410

401. Intangibility

402. Barkley the Dog Butler

403. Morrissey

404. John Larroquette

405. Come Together

406. Richard Dreyfuss

407. The Lost Weekend

408. Foghat

409. I Get Around

410. Bolero

Questions 411-420

411. In what movie did Peter Benchley play a reporter reporting from Amity Island?

412. "Cherry Pie" is the title track from whose album, released in 1990?

413. Which Broadway musical is about a 19 year old performer at the "Kit Kat Klub" and her relationship with an American writer?

414. Which eighth, youngest and most treacherous Koopaling makes his debut in the video game "Super Mario Sunshine" as the mastermind behind the evil Shadow Mario?

415. This Broadway musical starred music legend Barbra Streisand singing songs such as "People" and "Don't Rain on My Parade."

416. Who released the song "Fill Me In" in 2000? This English singer-songwriter became popular when featured on the single "Re-Rewind" by Artful Dodger in 1999.

417. It's the name of Zed's chopper in the 1994 film "Pulp Fiction."

418. It was John Cleese's name in the 1998 comedy film, "A Fish Called Wanda."

419. Who released the song "Foreclosure of a Dream" in 1992? This heavy metal song includes the infamous 1988 quote by George H. W. Bush, "Read my lips."

420. This 1995 film starring Bill Pullman and Sandra Bullock used the tagline, "A story about love at second sight."

Answers 411-420

411. Jaws

412. Warrant

413. Cabaret

414. Bowser, Jr.

415. Funny Girl

416. Craig David

417. Grace

418. Archie Leach

419. Megadeth

420. While You Were Sleeping

Questions 421-430

421. "Oceans, rivers, lakes and streams have all been touched by man. The poison floating out to sea, now threatens life on land," is a warning from which Beach Boys song?

422. This actor was originally cast to play Marty McFly in the 1985 film "Back to the Future," but the filmakers decided he was miscast and re-approached Michael J. Fox.

423. Who released the song "Fifty Ways To Leave Your Lover" in 1975?

424. When a song, book or other work that can be copyrighted is no longer protected by copyright, it is now in what area from which people may record and perform free of charge?

425. Which Broadway musical set in early 19th-Century France saw a revival in 2006 with another 463 performances?

426. What 2008 Woody Allen film did Penelope Cruz win the Oscar for Best Supporting Actress?

427. Name the 2000 movie starring Billy Crudup and Kate Hudson that this quote comes from, "The only true currency in this bankrupt world is what you share with someone else when you're uncool."

428. On Halloween in 1938, what novel did Orson Welles read over the radio to convince thousands of people that Earth was being invaded by Martians?

429. What "-gate" erupted when Taylor Swift's acceptance speech for Best Female Video at the 2009 MTV Video Music Awards was interrupted?

430. Who won the Best Engineered Recording: Special Or Novel Effects Grammy for a cover album of Beatles songs in 1964?

Answers 421-430

421. Don't Go Near the Water

422. Eric Stoltz

423. Paul Simon

424. Public Domain

425. Les Miserables

426. Vicky Christina Barcelona

427. Almost Famous

428. War of the Worlds

429. Kanyegate

430. The Chipmunks

Questions 431-440

431. Which sarcastic, but well-traveled chef joined "Top Chef: All-stars" Season 8 as a judge?

432. What band is fronted by vocalist and guitarist Johnny Rzeznik? They're well known for the songs "Iris" and "Name."

433. Who released the song "Man Overboard" in 2000? This band's 1999 multi-platinum album, "Enema of the State," reached #9 on the Billboard 200.

434. Which larger than life star asked, "Why don't you come up and see me sometime?" in the movie "She Done Him Wrong?"

435. Usually with a taste for Asian food, this giant lizard terrorized New York in 1998, only to be thwarted by the valiant efforts of Matthew Broderick.

436. What 1934 film was the first to win Academy Awards in all five major categories: Best Picture, Best Actor, Best Actress, Best Director and Best Screenplay, Adapted?

437. Who released the song "Grew up at Midnight" in 2012? This band is named after a Jewish rebel army that took control of Judea around 164 B.C.E.

438. Who voiced Moses and God in the animated film "The Prince of Egypt?"

439. He tells Officer Michaels he's old enough to party in the film "Superbad."

440. Claudia Wells played this character in the 1985 film "Back to the Future." However, she was replaced by Elizabeth Shue in the sequels.

Answers 431-440

431. Anthony Bourdain

432. The Goo Goo Dolls

433. blink-182

434. Mae West

435. Godzilla

436. It Happened One Night

437. The Maccabees

438. Val Kilmer

439. Fogel

440. Jennifer Parker

Questions 441-450

441. What word generally refers to a female singer with the highest vocal range?

442. The Muppet Babies actually made their live-action premiere two months before the animated series aired in what 1984 movie?

443. What Disney film remake starred Jamie Lee Curtis and Lindsey Lohan?

444. Angie Harmon voiced the Commisioner Barbara Gordon on what animated series?

445. Who released the song "Leonard" in 2012? "Tramp" is the third album by this American singer-songwriter who was born and raised in New Jersey.

446. Which 1988-1994 cartoon series was based on the comic strip of the same name by Jim Davis, featuring Jon, Orson, Binky the Clown, Dr. Liz, Wade Duck, Sheldon, Mort & Nermal?

447. What character on the TV sitcom "Friends" created a comic book about the adventures of "Science Boy"when he was a young?

448. What TV spy had the code names Bluebird, Freelancer, Mountaineer and Phoenix over the course of the show's five seasons?

449. John Turturro based a chracter in Miller's Crossing on the cinematographer of the movie. Can you name this cinematographer, who would go on to direct Men in Black?

450. Michael Keaton, Gedde Watanabe and George Wendt star in this 1986 comedy about a Japanese company taking over an American automotive plant.

Answers 441-450

441. Soprano

442. Muppets Take Manhattan

443. Freaky Friday

444. Batman Beyond

445. Sharon Van Etten

446. Garfield & Friends

447. Ross

448. Sydney Bristow

449. Barry Sonnenfeld

450. Gung Ho

Questions 451-460

451. He played the hotheaded jock, Charles Jefferson, whose car was wrecked by Spicoli but painted with slurs to look as if it was stolen by a rival high school in "Fast Times at Ridgemont High."

452. What British-American actress was once called the "greatest movie star of all" by biographer William J. Mann? She won two Academy Awards for Best Actress before passing away in 2011.

453. What animated TV show's theme song is "You've Got A Lot to See"?

454. What famous father may have been exposed to a little too much blood on the set of "Rambo: First Blood" such that he named his child Sage Moonblood?

455. What is the only "Star Trek" TV spin-off that has a theme song with lyrics sung during the opening credits?

456. He plays Derek Morgan on the TV show "Criminal Minds."

457. Who released the song "Landslide" in 1975? This song and "Rhiannon" were the first contributions to this band by Stevie Nicks.

458. What legendary rock band was comprised of John Bonham, John Paul Jones, Jimmy Page and Robert Plant?

459. She expressed regret later in life for removing her red bikini top for the excited Judge Reinhold in "Fast Times at Ridgemont High."

460. In the third of the Rocky movies, "Rocky III," Mr. T. portrays this fierce heavyweight boxer who knocks Rocky out in the second round of their first match.

Answers 451-460

451. Forest Whitaker

452. Elizabeth Taylor

453. Family Guy

454. Sylvester Stallone

455. Enterprise

456. Shemar Moore

457. Fleetwood Mac

458. Led Zeppelin

459. Phoebe Cates

460. James "Clubber" Lang

Questions 461-470

461. He stars as Mr. Holland in the 1995 film "Mr. Holland's Opus."

462. What video game is known as "Biohazzard" in Japan?

463. What "M*A*S*H" character was based on a Korean War nurse with a similar lusty nickname?

464. Who did Anna Anderson claim to be after attempting suicide in Berlin in 1920?

465. Homer frightens Bart by bursting into his room with a chainsaw and hockey mask during the episode called "Cape Feare" where Bart is hunted for revenge by which former Krusty the Clown sidekick?

466. What Beatles album is most often referred to as "The White Album?"

467. Who reportedly heard Snoop Dogg rap for the first time at a bachelor party?

468. The founders of the New York Giants and Pittsburg Steelers are also the great grandfathers of what "Girl with the Dragon Tatoo" actress?

469. What is the name of Chris Moltisanti's gangster-horror movie he wants to produce on the HBO series "The Sopranos"?

470. This cartoon character is on Dave McFly's shirt in the photo Marty carries in his wallet in "Back to the Future."

Answers 461-470

461. Richard Dreyfuss

462. Resident Evil

463. Margaret Houlihan

464. Anastasia

465. Sideshow Bob

466. The Beatles

467. Dr. Dre

468. Rooney Mara

469. Cleaver

470. Mickey Mouse

Questions 471-480

471. Who released the song "Diamonds & Rust" in 1975?

472. Who released the song "Gang Bang" in 2012?

473. Who released the song "The Ground Beneath Her Feet" in 2000? Please tell her not to step on the potatoes in case there's another famine!

474. What was Sam Malone's nickname on "Cheers?"

475. What show's first airing was on a 6-second delay because the network was afraid George Carlin might say something offensive?

476. Who released the song "Just Call Me Lonesome" in 1992?

477. This famous Kansas Citian is an actor, comedian and USMC Reserve officer best known for his work as a correspondent on Comedy Central's "The Daily Show."

478. Who released the song "Revengeance" in 2012? This group was created Max Cavalera after he left Sepultura.

479. "When Doves Cry" and "Let's Go Crazy" were hits from the soundtrack to what 1984 film starring Prince?

480. Who released the song "Dinosaurs will Die" in 2000? This American punk rock band became popular with their 1994 album "Punk in Drublic."

Answers 471-480

471. Joan Baez

472. Madonna

473. U2

474. Mayday

475. Saturday Night Live

476. Radney Foster

477. Rob Riggle, Jr.

478. Soulfly

479. Purple Rain

480. NoFX

Questions 481-490

481. What expansion team's first appearance in the Madden NFL video game franchise was in "Madden NFL 97?"

482. This actor, one of the most decorated of all time, won five of his Emmy Awards playing the same character on two different TV series.

483. What film used the tagline, "You won't believe your eye?"

484. Who released the song "Hairspray Queen" in 1992?

485. Who wrote the 1991 classic film "Thelma and Louise" featuring a then unheard-of Brad Pitt as a tantalizing piece of man candy for Susan Sarandon and Geena Davis?

486. At least one of those mean-spirited balcony berators on "The Muppet Show" is married. Also taking her name from a famous New York Hotel (and a section of Queens), what is Waldorf's wife's name?

487. Who released the song "Miner At The Dial-A-View" in 2000?

488. Who released the song "Here Comes The Rain Again" in 1983?

489. What is the name of Rudy Youngblood's character in Mel Gibson's film "Apocalypto?"

490. The Teen Angels (Brenda, Dee Dee and Taffy) go on mystery-solving adventures with what friend, whom the girls discovered and thawed from a block of ice, in the 1977 cartoon with his name in it?

Answers 481-490

481. Baltimore Ravens

482. Ed Asner

483. Monsters, Inc.

484. Nirvana

485. Callie Khouri

486. Astoria

487. Grandaddy

488. Eurythmics

489. Jaguar Paw

490. Captain Caveman

Questions 491-500

491. Whose interior design company is located at the Puck Building at 295 Lafayette St. in New York?

492. Who released the song "Gloria: In Excelsis Deo" in 1975? "Horses" was the debut studio album for this artist, who was a major influence on the New York punk rock scene.

493. What 1987 Steven Spielberg film tells the tale of an English boy captured by the Japanese in China during World War II?

494. Who released the song "Spit It Out" in 1999?

495. This jam band, fronted by Trey Anastasio, released "The Mango Song" off their fifth studio album "A Picture of Nectar."

496. What film tells the story of two young children, Brooke Shields and Christopher Atkins, marooned on a tropical island paradise in the South Pacific?

497. Who released the song "Wherever You Are" in 2012? This artist is part of Young Money Entertainment, a record label founded by rapper Lil Wayne.

498. What 1996 Vince Vaughn film was "so money"?

499. Who released the song "Magdalena" in 2000? This album, "Mer de Noms," debuted at #4 on the Billboard 200, which was one of the highest ever for a rock band's debut album.

500. This actress played Chandler Bing's father on "Friends."

Answers 491-500

491. Grace Adler

492. Patti Smith

493. Empire of the Sun

494. Slipknot

495. Phish

496. Blue Lagoon

497. Lil Twist

498. Swingers

499. A Perfect Circle

500. Kathleen Turner

Questions 501-510

501. Who first recorded the blues standard "Sweet Home Chicago" in the 1930s?

502. What film used the tagline, "Dishes. Relationships. Wind. This guy breaks everything?"

503. Who released the song "Take Off Your Shoes" in 2012? This visually iconic Irish singer-songwriter rose to fame in the late 1980s with her debut album "The Lion and the Cobra."

504. "You know I work all day to get you money to buy you things and it's worth it just to hear you say you're gonna give me everything," is from which Beatles song?

505. Who released the song "The Warmth" in 1999?

506. This tavern, featured on an old-time radio show was, "Where the elite meet to eat."

507. Who released the song "For the Record" in 2012? The fourth album, "Voyageur," by this Canadian singer includes guest appearances by Francis and the Lights, Norah Jones, Stornoway and John Roderick.

508. This 1984 film starring Emilio Estevez used the tagline, "It's 4 A.M. Do you know where your car is?"

509. Who released the song "Listen To The Radio (Atmospherics)" in 1983? This British artist is known for his hits "Glad to Be Gay," "2-4-6-8 Motorway" and "Don't Take No for an Answer."

510. Named for two New York City hotels, these crabby critics have belittled "The Muppets" from the balcony for years. What are their names?

Answers 501-510

501. Robert Johnson

502. Drop Dead Fred

503. Sinead O'Connor

504. A Hard Day's Night

505. Incubus

506. Duffy's

507. Kathleen Edwards

508. Repo Man

509. Tom Robinson

510. Statler & Waldorf

Questions 511-520

511. Which character in "Zombieland" is the only name that is not a state capital?

512. He's the real-life New York political figure who introduced the interim District Attorney on "Law & Order."

513. What sport does Sue's cheerleading team support on the ABC show "The Middle?"

514. What MGM production tied Disney's "Silly Symphonies" as the theatrical animated series with the most Academy Awards?

515. Hey hey hey! What 1972-1985 animated series was created, produced and hosted by comedian Bill Cosby? He also lent his voice to a number of characters, including the title character.

516. What 1957 Ingmar Bergman film features a medieval knight playing a game of chess against Death?

517. Brothers Malcolm and Angus Young founded what hard rock band?

518. What Japanese video game designer is credited with creating the "Super Mario Bros." universe?

519. Which Broadway musical, originally performed in December of 1981, follows the story of a trio of females singers from Chicago known as the "Dreamettes?"

520. What software company developed the game "StarCraft?"

Answers 511-520

511. Wichita

512. Rudolph Giuliani

513. Wrestling

514. Tom & Jerry

515. Fat Albert

516. The Seventh Seal

517. AC/DC

518. Shigeru Miyamoto

519. Dreamgirls

520. Blizzard

Questions 521-530

521. The 2008 inspirational football film was about the college career of Ernie Davis, the first African American to win the Heisman Trophy.

522. "Hey, ho, let's go!" is from which of The Ramones songs?

523. New Order recorded this 1982 dance hit which asks, "How does it feel to treat me like you do?" which was covered by Orgy in 1998.

524. She won an Academy Award for her portrayal of factory worker Norma Rae. Name the actress who played this role.

525. What type of dog was Rachael Ray's dog, Isaboo?

526. According to the song "Eastbound and Down," in what city was the beer located?

527. Who released the song "Suitcase" in 2012? She began working on her debut album when she was eleven years old.

528. Who released the song "At Seventeen" in 1975?

529. Betty White, Bridget Fonda and Bill Pullman get menaced by this giant animal in 1999's "Lake Placid."

530. Who released the song "Run On" in 1999?

Answers 521-530

521. The Express

522. Blitzkrieg Bop

523. Blue Monday

524. Sally Field

525. Pit Bull

526. Texarkana

527. Emeli Sandé

528. Janis Ian

529. Crocodile

530. Moby

Questions 531-540

531. Which pencil and paper game is called naughts and crosses in the UK?

532. Who released the song "You've Got It" in 2012? This artist's body of work has spanned from main-stream rock albums to folk-oriented, somber melodies.

533. What 1948 film was the first in the "Walt Disney True-Life Adventure" series?

534. In the film "Breakfast at Tiffany's," this character had a cat named "Cat."

535. Whose 1994 "Cracked Rear View" album sold 16 million copies in the U.S.?

536. Spongebob Squarepants has a pet snail named what?

537. On the TV show "Criminal Minds," what's the name of the suspect who shot and killed Aaron Hotchner's wife?

538. Who released the song "Oh My Sweet Carolina" in 2000? This alt-country/rock singer-songwriter from North Carolina left Whiskeytown to release his first solo album, "Heartbreaker" in 2000.

539. What was the name of the bottlenose dolphin portrayed in the television series created in 1964 by Ivan Tors?

540. Dann Florek portrayed this character on the TV show "Law & Order: SVU."

Answers 531-540

531. Tic-tac-toe

532. Bruce Springsteen

533. Seal Island

534. Holly Golightly

535. Hootie & the Blowfish

536. Gary

537. Reaper

538. Ryan Adams

539. Flipper

540. Don Cragan

Questions 541-550

541. Who released the song "Jive Talkin'" in 1975? This group was founded in 1958 with brothers Barry, Robin and Maurice Gibb.

542. It won seven Academy Awards in 1963, but this nearly four hour movie had no women in speaking roles. Which movie was it?

543. What word generally refers to a male singer with the highest vocal range?

544. The Grammy for Best Hard Rock/Metal Performance Vocal or Instrumental was only ever awarded one time, in 1989, which created controversy in the validity of the award when what unlikely band ousted favorite Metallica for the win?

545. In the final scene with Elizabeth and the Monster, her hairstyle, very tall with long white streaks running through it, pays homage to what earlier movie?

546. Who released the song "Aspenglow" in 1975?

547. This editor for "Food & Wine Magazine" is a regular judge for "Top Chef."

548. Where does Frasier follow Charlotte in the series finale of "Frasier?"

549. What is the name of Donald Duck's sister?

550. In the 1985 movie "Back to the Future," Doc Brown steals plutonium from terrorists of what country?

Answers 541-550

541. Bee Gees

542. Lawrence of Arabia

543. Tenor

544. Jethro Tull

545. Bride of Frankenstein

546. John Denver

547. Gail Simmons

548. Chicago

549. Della Duck

550. Libya

Questions 551-560

551. This Australian band, with a Kiwi frontman, who had hits with "Something So Strong" and "Don't Dream It's Over," released the single "Pineapple Head" off their fourth album Together Alone.

552. Who released the song "Jerk-Off" in 1992?

553. What does the job title "Q" stand for in the James Bond movies?

554. Who released the song "The Dolphin's Cry" in 1999? This band became a regular on the radio with its 1994 album, "Throwing Copper."

555. What cranky star of "Curb Your Enthusiasm" stars as the cranky Boris Yellnikoff in Woody Allen's "Whatever Works"?

556. This 1969 romantic comedy film starring Richard Benjamin and Ali MacGraw used the tagline, "Every father's daughter is a virgin."

557. According to the Beatles' song "Being For The Benefit Of Mr. Kite", who will dance the waltz of course?

558. This 1995 animated film tells the story of a pig who wants to be a sheepdog, an adaptation from a 1983 novel called "The Sheep-Pig."

559. On the sitcom "Seinfeld," library investigator Lt. Bookman pursued Jerry to recover which book by Norman Mailer that he checked out over 20 years earlier?

560. Upon finding a Hummer filled with guns, what does Woody Harrelson's character, Tallahassee, thank God for in the film "Zombieland?"

Answers 551-560

551. Crowded House

552. Tool

553. Quartermaster

554. Live

555. Larry David

556. Goodbye, Columbus

557. Henry the Horse

558. Babe

559. Tropic of Cancer

560. Rednecks

Questions 561-570

561. Name the 1984 movie starring Tom Hanks and Daryl Hannah that this quote comes from, "I don't understand. All my life I've been waiting for someone and when I find her, she's a fish."

562. "The Smurfs" feature the characters Papa Smurf, Smurfette, the evil Gargamel and his cat. What's Gargamel's cat's name?

563. What band released the album "A Crow Left of the Murder" in 2004?

564. What British electronica group's 1995 debut album was "Exit Planet Dust?"

565. This ball-balancing Koopaling from "Super Mario Bros. 3" shares his name with the frontman from the rock band Motorhead.

566. What 2003 film, starring Diane Lane, was about a recently divorced woman who moved to Italy and began rebuilding a villa?

567. What's the highest bill denomination in the standard classic U.S. version of Monopoly?

568. In the TV show "Heroes," Micah Sanders could manipulate technology through a special form of electrical or telekinetic manipulation. What is this called?

569. What Rodgers and Hart "you left me standing alone" song has been covered by Mel Torme, Elvis Presley, Less Than Jake and perhaps, most famously, The Marcels.

570. "Love is in the hair," was the tagline for this 1998 comedy film starring Cameron Diaz, Matt Dillon and Ben Stiller.

Answers 561-570

561. Splash

562. Azrael

563. Incubus

564. The Chemical Brothers

565. Lemmy Koopa

566. Under the Tuscan Sun

567. 500

568. Technopathy

569. Blue Moon

570. There's Something About Mary

Questions 571-580

571. Who released the song "On A Night Like This" in 2000?

572. Who released the song "Absolutely (Story of a Girl)" in 2000?

573. This comic strip character wrote "The Adventures of Angry Bob."

574. This 1983 comedy film starring Dan Aykroyd and Eddie Murphy used the tagline, "They're not just getting rich. They're getting even."

575. What 1981 horror movie's songs all contain the word "moon" in the titles?

576. In 1999's "The Mummy," Evelyn and Imhotep both use the phrase, "Death is only the," what?

577. Which R.E.M. songs asks, "You don't really love that guy you make it with now do you? I know you don't love that guy cause I can see right through you. I am, I am, I am," who?

578. "In the time of chimpanzees I was a monkey," is the opening line of what song?

579. This classic film used the tagline, "Every man dies, not every man really lives."

580. What year saw "Psycho," "Spartacus," and "Exodus" released in theaters?

Answers 571-580

571. Kylie Minogue

572. Nine Days

573. Rat

574. Trading Places

575. American Werewolf in London

576. Beginning

577. Superman

578. Loser

579. Braveheart

580. 1960

Questions 581-590

581. Who released the song "Roman Holiday" in 2012? In 2010, this artist was the first female solo artist to have seven singles on the Billboard Hot 100 at the same time.

582. Roderick Kingsley, fashion designer and billionaire, discovered the lair of Norman Osborn and used his Green Goblin sled to become this "Spider-Man" villain.

583. Who released the song "Come Healing" in 2012? Not just a musician, this artist published a book of poetry, "Let Us Compare Mythologies," in 1956.

584. What is the name of bluegrass singer Alison Krauss' backup band?

585. What "Terminator 2" robot is made of a metallic poly-alloy superfluid that can form itself and any shape?

586. This 2008 Hayao Miyazaki cartoon re-imagined "The Little Mermaid" fairy tale as a magical goldfish who befriends a 5-year-old boy named Sosuke and wants to become a real girl.

587. Who stars as FBI agent Carl Hanratty in the Steven Spielberg film "Catch Me If You Can"?

588. Who released the song "Stuck In A Moment You Can't Get Out Of" in 2000? I'm sure the lead singer of this band is part of some worldwide foundation to get you unstuck.

589. Who released the song "He's Simple, He's Dumb, He's the Pilot" in 2000?

590. What part in "Airplane!" did David Letterman audition for?

Answers 581-590

581. Nicki Minaj

582. Hobgoblin

583. Leonard Cohen

584. Union Station

585. T-1000

586. Ponyo

587. Tom Hanks

588. U2

589. Grandaddy

590. Ted Striker

Questions 591-600

591. What werewolf film used the tagline, "Things are about to get a little hairy?"

592. Who released the song "Bitch School" in 1992?

593. "Once upon a time there were three little girls who went to the police academy," was the opening line for what popular TV series?

594. Which actress was 85 years-old when she starred in the film "Sextet?"

595. Who released the song "Sexx Laws" in 1999? This alt-rock artist has been hailed as one of the most creative musicians of the 1990s and 2000s.

596. What film used the tagline, "A girl wilder than a peach orchard hog?"

597. Who released the song "Konstantine" in 2000? Their first single, "If You C Jordan," was one of the most successful by this Orange County, CA, band formed in 1998.

598. Who released the song "Leather" in 1992?

599. Who released the song "The Matador" in 2012? This singer-songwriter has composed hits for Anne Murray, Etta James, George Strait, Martina McBride, Neil Diamond, Patty Loveless and Trisha Yearwood.

600. What famous songwriter and singer plays Tony Lacey in Woody Allen's film "Annie Hall"?

Answers 591-600

591. American Werewolf in Paris

592. Spinal Tap

593. Charlie's Angels

594. Mae West

595. Beck

596. The Girl from Tobacco Row

597. Something Corporate

598. Tori Amos

599. Gretchen Peters

600. Paul Simon

Questions 601-610

601. This film director's tombstone reads "I'm in on a plot."

602. Ray Parker, Jr. wrote the title song for "Ghostbusters" after hearing a commercial jingle. Huey Lewis and the News disagreed, citing the similarities between the movie theme and which one of their earlier hits?

603. Who released the song "Let's Get Rocked" in 1992?

604. "I've always been in love with you. I guess you've always known it's true," are lyrics in which Madonna song?

605. Which of the "Top Chef" judges casts out the weakest contestant by uttering, "Pack your knives and go?"

606. Who released the song "A New England" in 1983? This artist spent three months in the British Army before he bought his way out.

607. Who retired from his radio show, "Letter From America," after 58 years?

608. What actor from "The Untouchables" turned down the lead role in "Raising Arizona" that eventually went to Nicolas Cage?

609. Who released the song "Rosa's Coronas" in 1999?

610. In what 1956 movie did Robby the Robot first appear?

Answers 601-610

601. Alfred Hitchcock

602. I Want a New Drug

603. Def Leppard

604. Take a Bow

605. Padma Lakshmi

606. Billy Bragg

607. Alistair Cooke

608. Kevin Costner

609. Kate Campbell

610. Forbidden Planet

Questions 611-620

611. What ad agency does Don Draper work for in the first season of "Mad Men."

612. This film didn't hide behind its tagline, "From zero to hero."

613. The Beatles sang, "Oh, please, say to me you'll let me be your man & please, say to me," what?

614. Who released the song "Insomnia" in 1999?

615. What was Padma Lakshmi's area of expertise before she began hosting "Top Chef?"

616. TV's Sugarbaker sisters ran their interior decorating firm from their home at 1521 Sycamore Street in Atlanta on what popular sitcom?

617. What's the player's character name in the "Grand Theft Auto: Vice City" game?

618. What director does Gwyneth Paltrow call Uncle Morty?

619. "Well, since my baby left me, I found a new place to dwell," is from what Elvis song?

620. In 1999, what album did Britney Spears debut, rocketing her into super-stardom? It would eventually become certified double platinum.

Answers 611-620

611. Sterling Cooper

612. The Mask

613. I Want To Hold Your Hand

614. Megadeth

615. Cookbook Author

616. Designing Women

617. Tommy Vercetti

618. Steven Spielberg

619. Heartbreak Hotel

620. Baby One More Time

Questions 621-627

621. Who released the song "The Heart of Rock 'n Roll" in 1983?

622. What Animal Planet program features Shorty Rossi?

623. Who directed an episode of "The Sopranos" titled "Pine Barrens" in 2001?

624. This long-running animated sitcom owns the title for most wins by any animated show of all time, with 27.

625. In what 1985 drama does a Philadelphia cop hides out in an Amish community to protect a young boy who saw a murder?

626. "I gave her my heart and she gave me a pen," is spouted by Lloyd Dobler in what 1989 John Hughes classic film?

627. What NBC late-night talk show host was the original host of MTV's "Total Request Live" (TRL)?

Answers 621-627

621. Huey Lewis & The News

622. Pit Boss

623. Steve Buscemi

624. The Simpsons

625. Witness

626. Say Anything

627. Carson Daly

ABOUT THE AUTHOR

Dr. Seven Phoenix (Doc) has hosted several popular pub trivia nights in Eugene, Oregon since early 2008. Seven Phoenix grew up in Pennsylvania, before moving to the Pacific Northwest, where he earned his Ph.D. in Sociology. Doc loves spending time with his English Mastiff, Kinsey, and enjoys hiking and exploring the Pacific Northwest (in the three months of the year when it isn't raining). You can email Doc at: Se7enPhoenix@gmail.com or follow him on twitter @Se7enPhoenix.

www.ingramcontent.com/pod-product-compliance
Lightning Source LLC
Chambersburg PA
CBHW071406280526
45787CB00001B/452